DAY (Look in the back of the book for the antonym.)

are words with the opposite meaning.

courageous

CLOSER TO

RIGHT PAGE

OUTSIDE

by Kim & Robert Rayevsky

HOLIDAY HOUSE / NEW YORK

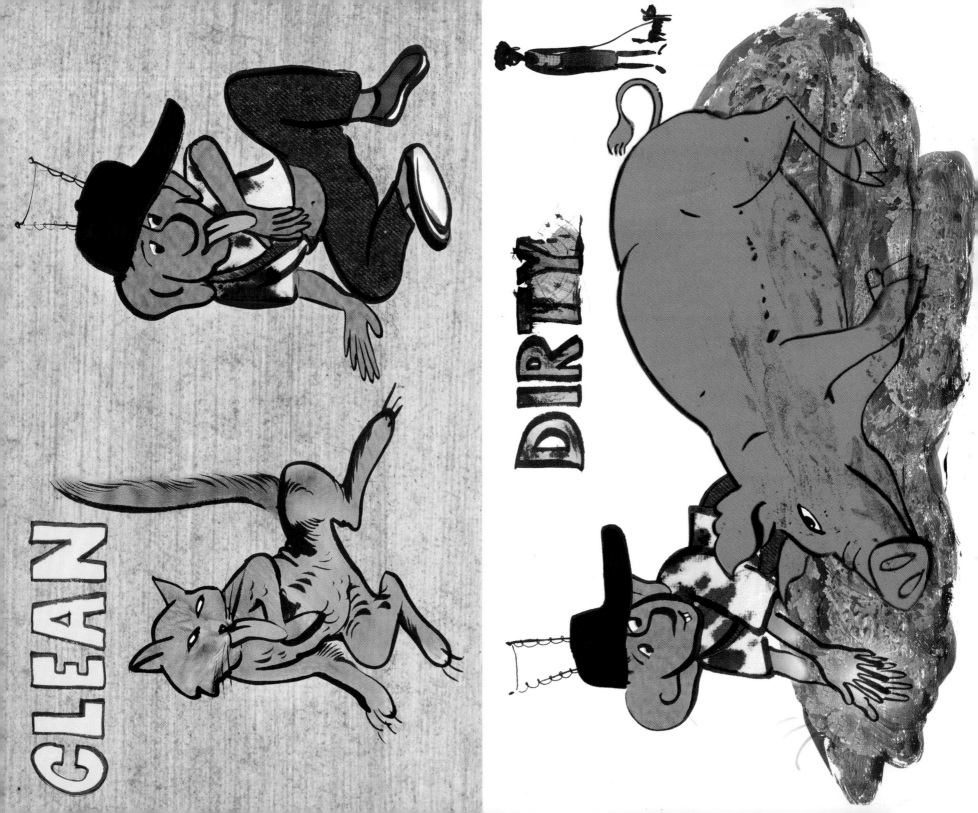

NEAT

ANTONYMS

ON THE TOP OF THE BUILDING

UNDER the mattresses

FRIENDLY

HOSTILE

FULL

EMPTY

REAL ANIMALS

ugly

awake

alert

asleep

Fantastic, MYTHOLOGICAL ANIMAL

Marcel Duchamp
Mona Lisa, 1919

Beautiful

UNCOLORED

BLACK and WHITE PICTURES

BIG HUGE

little small tiny

HATTED

HATLESS

standing

sitting

LONELINESS

COMPANIONSHIP

Leonardo da Vinci
Mona Lisa, 1503–

OBEDIENT-DISOBEDIENT

GIVE

TAKE

COLD

HOT

safety

DANGER!!!

LIGHT background

DARK background

FEMALE SYMBOL

MALE SYMBOL

WOMAN

MAN

casual dressed down

Dressed up

BEARDED

beardless

small beard

Medium-sized beard

COLORED

PICTURES

HUNGRY!!!

ABSTRACT PICTURE

realistic picture

Surrealistic picture

underweight lean skinny slim slender

BIG beard

FULL

FAT overweight

SYNONYMS

are different words that have the same meaning.

LIMOUSINE

AUTOMOBILE

VEHICLE

WHEELS

car

ARGUE
FIGHT
Squabble
quarrel
COMPLAIN
dispute
BICKER

SYNONYMS

HOUSE
HOME

road
street

bug insect

LARGE

tremendous

SEE LOOK

WATCH

thorny

bristly

Seafood

pretty handsome
attractive beautiful
pleasing

prickly spiny

Sharp

Synonyms

teacher
professor

ARCHITECTURE
structure

building

construction

abominable
repulsive
repugnant
disgusting
DETESTABLE
abhorrent
HIDEOUS

SCARED
afraid
shocked
terrified
chilled
FRIGHTENED

HUGE

monster
beast

GIANT

FISH

LITTLE
tiny

bounds
VAULTS
hurdles
SPRINGS
bounces
Jumps
leaps

teenager   ADOLESCENT

YOUTH

laugh
giggle
titter
chuckle

SKETCHES
Doodles

drawings

AMITY
tranquility

PEACE

HARMONY
UNION
CONCORD
UNITY
friendship
truce

HOMONYMS

- are words that have the same sound and sometimes the same spelling, but different meanings.

I **HEAR** music, so **HERE** I am
all dressed up for the party.

WHERE'S my hat?

My puppy WEARS my hat!

TOW a bus with a TOE

I MISSED my mommy!

NIGHT

Printed in the United States of America
www.holidayhouse.com
First Edition
1 3 5 7 9 10 8 6 4 2

Library of Congress Cataloging-in-Publication Data
Rayevsky, Kim.
Antonyms, synonyms, & homonyms / by Kim and Robert Rayevsky.—1st ed.
p. cm.
ISBN-13: 978-0-8234-1889-3 (hardcover)
ISBN-10: 0-8234-1889-8 (hardcover)
1. English language—Synonyms and antonyms—Juvenile literature.
2. English language—Homonyms—Juvenile literature. I. Rayevsky, Robert.
II. Title.

PE1591.R39 2006
428.1—dc22
2005035846

The image of Leonardo Da Vinci's *Mona Lisa* is used with permission
of Harley Hahn at www.harley.com.

The image of Marcel Duchamp's *Mona Lisa LHOOQ* is used with permission
of © 2006 Artists Rights Society (ARS), New York / ADAGP, Paris / Succession
Marcel Duchamp.

The image of Charlie Chaplin is used with permission of the Roy Export
Company Establishment.